Information Technology & Insights: Information Systems for Decision Making

---

Bringing a Vision and Understanding to Effective Practices

The Erudite Collection: Volume 1

Copyright © 2018 R. Allen Conner
All rights reserved.

All rights reserved. No part of this publication may be reproduced, distributed, or transmitted in any form or by any means, including photocopying, recording, or other electronic or mechanical methods, without the prior written permission of the publisher, except in the case of brief quotations embodied in critical reviews and certain other noncommercial uses permitted by copyright law.

3

CONTENTS

CONTENTS 4
INTRODUCTION 6
Information Management 7
Data Analytics 7
    Data Analytics Overview 7
    Advantages & Disadvantages of Data Analytics 2 8
    Challenges of Implementing Data Analytics 9
    Transformation 9
    The Trend of Data Analytics 9
    [Insight]: Management Concerns 10
Information Management, Data, and Infrastructure 10
    The Future of Information Technology 10
    Impact of IT Architecture 11
    Data Storage Methods 12
    [Insight]: Network Structures and Data Warehouses 12
Enterprises and Cyber Security 13
    Fundamental Challenges 13
    Target 14
    Why the Attack Transpired 15
[Insight]: Cybersecurity Posture and Governance 15
[Insight]: e-Commerce 16
Wireless and Mobile Tech 17
    What is Wireless and Mobile Technology 17
    Mobile and Wireless Technologies: Examining D-Airlines 18
    Mobile and Wireless Technologies: Examining V-Airlines 18
    Efficiency 19
    Operational and Enterprise Systems 19
[Insight]: Wireless and Mobile 20
[Insight]: Conduct and Ethics 20
[Insight]: Fraud and Risk Factors 21
[Insight]: Visualization Technologies 22

[Insight]: Project Management and SDLC 22
IT Strategic Plan: Exploring Cab Technology Platforms 23
    Introduction 23
    Technology and Security 23
    Personnel 24
    SWOT Analysis 25
    Strategic Plan 26
BIBLIOGRAPHY 28

INTRODUCTION

Focusing on industry best practices while including some of the most bleeding edge methodologies, Information Technology & Insights: The Erudite Collection helps to build students and professional's competency, assessment skills, and talent.

The Erudite Collection is brimming with checklists and procedures; this book enables you to put these new insights into action immediately. The book outlines IT processes in detail, allowing the student or professional to acquire the necessary skills, a greater understanding of roles, and a profound view of technology deployments.

The book teaches practical techniques that will be used on a daily operational basis while furthering the readers understanding by using examples in the form of case studies titled Insights throughout the collection. Information Technology & Insights: The Erudite Collection will be a valuable resource for Information Technology professionals who wear various hats and IT students.

Information Management

Information technology has changed the concept of the way we do business over the years and is continuing to improve business interactions significantly. Information Technology influences the way organizations conduct operations to be efficient and as productive as possible. IT also engages in issues that include management. This process enables corrective measures for problems which might not have been addressed, or resolved separately, causing a more significant effect or temporary fix.

The healthcare industry is probably where enterprise architecture seems the most relevant. Many divisions of healthcare do not effectively communicate with each other as a result of the broken enterprise architecture. Establishments are creating and improving new ways to keep track better and maintain patient information. Along with these collaborative issues, security comes into play. The hierarchy from collaboration down to safety is an ever-present obstacle hindering organizational information.

Technology is developing at such a degree that once we are comfortable with certain facets, new levels of orientation/deployments or infrastructures are produced. The target is a continuous goal, but with human resourcefulness, the more we progress so does the target design.

Competitive gain is achieved by providing a product/service in a way that customers value more than the competitions. Information technology gives a company that viable advantage. Innovation generates ways to do things in new and creative ideas which drive the target architecture forward.

Data Analytics

Data Analytics Overview

Business intelligence and analytics along with the related field of big data analytics have become progressively essential in both the educational and the business communities over the past two decades (Hsinchun, 2012). Data analytics are the qualitative/quantitative methods, and practices performed to improve productivity and business achievement. Data is extracted and classified to identify interactive patterns and techniques which differ regarding organizational requirements. Data analytics are predominantly conducted in a business-to-consumer relationship. Global establishments accumulate and analyze data associated with customers, processes, and market economics. Data is classified, analyzed, and then stored for the studying of procuring trends.

Data that constantly changes simplifies decision-making. A social networking website as an example accumulates data associated with end-user preferences and interests according to demographics, age, and gender. An accurate analysis reveals patterns and enables the sites arrangement of content, design and general strategy.

Advantages & Disadvantages of Data Analytics 2

Google was among the first companies to research with big data. Google developed ways of determining proof while performing small-scale projects to learn if analytical models could enhance with new sources of input. The results of their research returned positive in most cases.

Analytics is no longer an experimental issue. Many organizations have begun to accomplish positive results, and are increasing their efforts to incorporate more data and models.

The advantages of data analytics consist of cost reduction, better decision making, and new products/services. Big data technologies and cloud analytics can provide considerable cost advantages. Comparisons between data analytics and traditional sources such as data warehouses are challenging because of functionality.

Data analytics has always included efforts to progress decision making. Large businesses are looking for ways to make faster and better decisions using analytics.

Remarkable uses of analytics are creating new products and services for customers. Online companies have been doing this for years. Primarily offline firms are joining in also. GE, for example, has made a significant investment in new service models for its industrial products using big data analytics (Davenport, 2014).

The usage of data within organizations can bring huge advantages, but like any other scenario, it has its limitations and disadvantages. Data analytics can be unaccommodating if site traffic is not substantial. It must also be explicitly configured to a user's liking which could have an adverse influence on performance and could present privacy concerns.

Data analytics is not precise with low traffic volume. The results displayed might not be correct due to visitor settings or configuration of the website. A statistically substantial amount of traffic is needed to show behavior patterns.

Challenges of Implementing Data Analytics

Many problems and obstacles that companies come across when utilizing data analytics accrue from not knowing the difference between big data analytics and business intelligence. Big data analytics is about extracting usable information from data which can give decision makers the insight to create data focused organizations. As a data-centric approach, BI&A has its roots in the long-standing database management field. It relies heavily on various data collection, extraction, and analysis technologies (Chaudhuri et al. 2011; Turban et al. 2008; Watson and Wixom 2007). Other challenges are as follows:

- Finding the right use cases
- Companies thinking that initializing analytics on an enormous set of data is BDA
- Overrating the analytics development of the organization

Transformation

A result of implementing data analytics into the Airbnb community marketplace improved vendor data to 90% while reducing tag deployment time using Google tag manager.

Airbnb is designed with a unified product team that cooperates on marketing projects. The company uses plenty of website tags, including a unique label for each of their multiple AdWords accounts and surplus tags for an array of vendors. Adwords accounts will accumulate a variety of statistics that are available through the Adwords reporting interface (Geddes, 2014). To avoid a bottleneck amongst the operations and marketing teams, they needed a management system. The first satisfactory was not successful due to the required add-ons, and the cost was too expensive.

After exploring options, the team opted to shift its tagging to Google. Many reasons contributed to the resolution. They already used numerous Google tools, so the team felt templates would enable a smooth integration. Also, Google's extensive QA and reporting features would make it easier to test and deploy. In the past, tagging was a complicated process that averaged a few days to complete.

The Trend of Data Analytics

The upcoming trends in the use of data analytics in marketing estate are very hopeful. The laborious procedure of checking the correctness of JavaScript tags and establishing QA before final deployment will come to an end. Tasks will be completed in a matter of hours after receiving a tag and moved to QA to be deployed. As time progresses, data such as the route customers take while traveling domestically and foreign will provide info for better strategic layouts, marketing, pricing.

[Insight]: Management Concerns

Business productivity and cost reduction are of primary concerns. Businesses focus predominantly on customer consummation. The services that are offered are aimed to meet the needs of the clients. When production increases, the cost to produce output decreases which play an essential part in the aptitude to be competitive. Broader margins mean higher profits for the company, measuring standards allows evaluation of the rates of productivity for employees.

IT reliability and efficiency refer to the concept that what a company can accomplish or achieve depends on what its IT team can do. The lack of a structured method to validate the underlying IT infrastructure leads to technical glitches and outages, which results in an unfriendly business impact. Cloud computing allows you to configure what is mostly a virtual office to give you the flexibility of communicating to your business anywhere, any time.

Businesses of all sizes are shifting to cloud computing environments to take advantage of the benefits. Cloud computing enables enterprises to scale compute and storage on an as-needed basis, which can keep costs low. Services are designed to be automated and self-provisioning, giving the end-users the ability to scale their needs without any manual intervention. It also provides the ability to enable employees to gain access to data and applications from anywhere, making them more productive on the go.

Information Management, Data, and Infrastructure

The Future of Information Technology

Data or information is the foundation of every organization. Businesses with correct, consistent and well-timed information have an advantage over many of their competitors. Best practices center around the concept that information should be treated the same as valuable assets. Assets need careful management, attentive governance, and tactical contemplation when dealing with their intended use and control.

Strategies organizations choose to conduct business are becoming more advanced; the challenges they face become more sophisticated as well. Information management is one of those obstacles. Over time data is continuously being produced and companies are tasked with managing and securing this critically essential information. Information management arranges the processed data in a way that increases the configuration in which data is portrayed. Information management deals with how data is stored and structured; and the speed at which it is captured, analyzed, and reported (Turban, 2012). By creating a design to organize data handling, the information is more manageable.

The opposite exists for organizations as well. Businesses that do not apply best practices to their information management procedures find that vital business information is not accessible when needed or worse, nowhere to be obtained when it is time for decisions to be made. When relevant data is unattainable or unable to be shared, it compromises the trust of the user community. Vital processes reliant on this information are the source of exceptions needing manual involvement and result in inadequacy and profit loss.

Skillful information management increases organizational proficiency and business outcomes by providing measurable benefits such as the customer's trust, optimization, risk mitigation, and internal transparency. Any business output that is reliant on the delivery of quality information to the right process on time in an understandable way needs well-oriented information management practices.

Impact of IT Architecture

Many organizations face growing pressure to become more competitive and proficient to meet expectations. These challenges are designed to help protect personal information, improve processes, and make organizational changes to support ways of conducting business. These challenges require a detailed understanding of the current architecture including capabilities, services, resources/risks, and plans to develop for future problems. Enterprise Architecture now takes risk-based approaches to help businesses achieve goals and accomplish objectives by evaluating tasks to govern the right level of investment to make in each.

An example would consist of a company in the chemical industry with a headquarters, a global sales unit, and some business units in other countries. Each business unit produces and also delivers specified products to the worldwide sales unit. As best practices, the company has chosen the information-driven principle for systems delineation. Common information was analyzed to create central systems, where different subsystems access and update this collective information. The company invested in an ERP system. The ERP consisted of a kernel containing all fundamental information on products, sales, warehouses, etc. When the system was implemented in different business units, local information could further be added.

The architectural design used in the company lead to an IT investment that must be centrally evaluated. The expansion, application, and operation of new systems must be viewed as a central infrastructural cost which is handled by the IT department. The fundamental responsibility of the IT department makes it easier to coordinate and control IT investment on a corporate level (Pessi, Magoulas, & Hugoson, 2011). IT architecture also impacts the effectiveness of information management by adding focus on productive roll-outs of the system, also covering education in how to operate the system.

Data Storage Methods

There are many means to store data, but databases and data warehousing would be preferred. Databases are essential because they store data generated by business apps, sensors, and transaction processing systems (Turban, 2012). Databases provide a well-organized way to store, retrieve and analyze data. System files function similarly to databases, but they are far less proficient. Databases are particularly crucial for business and research. Storing information in a database would allow on-demand details when dealing with the various chemicals, global shipping, and numerical measures as examples.

Another storage method which could be evaluated is data warehouses. Data warehouses would be of use to the chemical industry because they combine data from multiple sources. Data warehousing can significantly improve son shipping demands. A certain amount of a particular chemical could be housed somewhere closer to a customer, which in turn, would increase shipping efficiency.

Of the two methods listed, data warehousing would be the optimal choice. By cross-referencing data collected on purchases, shipping and production, costs can be significantly reduced while optimizing shipping and physical storage along with maintenance of chemicals as reflected by the example.

[Insight]: Network Structures and Data Warehouses

There are three leading types of IT processing involved in the administration of a business. Business collaboration processing, business intelligence, and business transaction. Collaboration systems allow business managers to share information about business operations. Business intelligence application analyzes those operations with the objective of making them efficient, while business transactions run day-to-day processes. Before integrating business intelligence, most companies

examined business operations using decision support applications. These applications conveyed directly on data stored in transaction databases. Many problems existed with this approach.
- Data was not typically in a suitable form for reporting
- Quality concerns
- Decision support degraded business transaction performance
- Information was spread transversely
- The absence of historical data.

Data warehousing was offered to solve these data and performance issues and primarily aimed to enhance business operating systems and performance.

Businesses collect data using various tools. When time studies are executed at the worker level, they can measure response time, and they can gather statistics on application response. With this data and analytics software, it's conceivable to apply BI ideologies to increase productivity.

Businesses that have adopted robust network infrastructures will already have a map of business procedures that link with IT applications. By combining information about operations, it is possible to calculate how the trade is running and how it can become more productive. Even where EA data is not available, the percentage of an industrial practice that forms an IT workflow can yield valuable insights.

Enterprises and Cyber Security

The protection of intellectual property from theft and exploitation is an increasingly severe management issue. The government has acknowledged cybersecurity as one of the most severe economic and security challenges nationwide. Companies today are tasked with defending the threat of cyber criminals along with disgruntled employees. The danger of those cybercriminals taking sensitive information, releasing intellectual property to rivals, or engaging in online fraud has increased intensely over the past few years. Many technologically advanced companies have fell victim to public breaches, while many instances go unreported.

Fundamental Challenges

Most large companies have strengthened their cybersecurity practices over the past few years. Proper processes have been applied to identify risks and develop mitigation policies. Desktop environments are not as wide open as they were many years ago. USB ports have been disabled, and Webmail services are also being blocked.

While value continues to transition into online transactions, it's creating more significant incentives for cybercriminals. Additionally, businesses looking to mine data for information, product launches, and market information, create intellectual property that is attractive to criminals.

Another challenge exists with supply chains, which have become more interlocked. Companies have encouraged vendors and customers to join their networks to strengthen ties and optimize those supply chains. This practice makes hardening a businesses networked environment almost impossible. Closer integration with business associates can provide benefits, but it also undermines a corporation's defense against attacks.

Target

During the peak of holiday shopping, Target said that up to 40 million customers' credit and debit card data had been copied from people who shopped in stores from Nov. 27 to Dec. 15 (Yang & Jayakumar, 2014). The first incident occurred on November 30, 2013, when malware gained access to U.S. staging points and then on Russian computers. Target was notified, but no actions were taken. On December 2, 2013, another version of the exfiltration malware was loaded which raised awareness again. For the second time, no operations were executed by Target.

Target had substantial reasons to investigate the integrity of their infrastructure. They did not have a firm position on their security environment proven by the lack of action on their part. Target had just implemented FireEye's monitoring software but was ignoring the notifications. If Target's security team had followed up on the earliest FireEye alerts, it could have been right behind the hackers on their escape path (Riley, Elgin, & Matlock, 2014).

Nevertheless, once aware of the breach, Target took a series of decisive actions. The company hired security experts at Verizon to test its infrastructure for weaknesses. The specialists were able to obtain access to the complete system once inside. Results showed that passwords were not being used in a manner that would give proper protection.

They overhauled their systems to identify internal and external risks to customers personal information and added additional training for employees dealing with the customer's safety. The company also announced it would upgrade to advanced registers and other technology to process new and safer cards. Target replaced all of their card machines with chip reading machines to add an extra layer of security. Target encouraged all the credit card companies to replace their credit cards with the chipped versions. The credit and debit cards most U.S. citizens use are shockingly vulnerable to fraud, relying on decades-old technology that makes them susceptible (Hardy, M. 2014). During the follow-up analysis, the consultant's saw significant improvements where only a few areas were able to be compromised. These areas which were secured within a few days.

Allowing expert's access gave the company a better view of their infrastructure and vulnerabilities. The follow up was as equally important. A second permitted penetration test for security tests to reinforce the policies, procedures, software, and changes.

Why the Attack Transpired
Many holes existed in their network which was brought forward by the consultant's analysis. Once the attackers gained access, they had privileges to exploit the whole infrastructure. A combination of lousy support and incompetent administration that disregarded notifications of a security threat aided in the success of the attack. If the warnings were addressed as received, and the proper actions and escalations executed at appropriate intervals, This incident could have been evaded.

Target appears to have accomplished many things since the crisis. Being able to function collectively during an event and returning to operational status is a primary essential component in today's business world. Ultimately, the plan of activities for Target to continue successfully will consist of maintaining an impressive security structure (2015). Much can be spent on security, but it's useless if you're not investing in the right assets. Many establishments don't take security seriously until they have been compromised.

[Insight]: Cybersecurity Posture and Governance
When regarding cybersecurity, organizations have begun to contemplate the issue as part of more substantial compliance rather than pushing cybersecurity matters to IT. When dealing with the outcome of public data breaches and losses of compromised businesses, corporate boards are now handling cybersecurity as a governance and risk management issue. 3 points that justify the impactful relationship are:

- Access: Deals with proper authentication credentials which allow retrieval of sensitive data.
- Policies: Acceptable use policy communications directed to employee's regarding responsibility and security.
- Password Recycling: Changing of credentials to reinforce security measures in case that data has been compromised allowing fraudulent behavior.

Other instances as client data and intellectual property fall under these guidelines as well.

Most organizations are heavily dependent on information technology from laptops, servers, desktops, tablets, and smartphones. An array of unfortunate episodes can disrupt these devices. The incidents range from power outages to data loss caused by misguided employees, or criminals.

During the Sony attack, cell phones, Gmail accounts, and notepads were used to keep operations running while Sony executives had to devise a 1:1 phone tree network to relay information to one another. Old Blackberry phones were also being used for communication efforts. The most basic business continuity requirement is to keep essential functions up and running during a disaster. A business continuity plan considers various unpredictable events such as fires, cyber attacks, and other external threats.

Networks are the backbones of information infrastructures. Continuity is essential for organizations of any size, but it may not be practical for any but the largest enterprises to maintain all functions for the duration of a disaster.

[Insight]: e-Commerce

The principal business advantages of e-business and e-commerce are the ability to sell products and services without the consumer having to visit the physical site while also being able to serve on a 24-hour basis. eCommerce enables the ability to gain revenue during closed hours. e-Commerce also allows for a more comprehensive customer range. The greatest strength, which is good for the consumer, provides for research of the service or product before purchase. The disadvantages of e-commerce are the lack of customer/sales relationship building. Another drawback is the increase in fraudulent activities due to the nature of online sales. E-commerce requires a great deal of security, and extensive infrastructure to properly function.

Availability is a key challenge faced by e-commerce. A sizeable adaptable infrastructure is needed to support online business. Traffic can become heavy at times and implementing updates for maintenance and security can become tedious. This obstacle can be overcome by incorporating third-party hosting so daily operations can run as efficiently as possible.

Privacy has become a significant issue as most companies have included e-commerce into their business structure. E-commerce usually tracks customer's data and retains personal information. An example of this would be cookies that are stored on your browser. Many sites let you know that cookies must be enabled to view or use.

Ethical and legal considerations:
- Sales Tax: Businesses must keep track of statewide regulatory laws which vary for each state
- Antitrust Laws: Derived for protecting consumers from malicious business practices

Wireless and Mobile Tech

What is Wireless and Mobile Technology

Wireless technologies use radio waves to connect with devices or networks designed to transmit and receive data. Adoption of these practices by consumers has allowed businesses to interact with them in a closer way.

Portable devices have become popular with users over past years. Smartphones, tablets, and eReaders have become efficient enough to replace computers for specific functions. These mobile devices provide the means that is increasingly vital to the way that people have chosen to interact.

The combination of wireless and mobile technologies has opened new methods for businesses to improve efficiency. There are numerous instances of companies that have capitalized on wireless technology to create fascinating advances.

Both allow employees to have real-time communication with the company and its operations while providing fast connectivity to vendors. They both also feature ways of marketing and commerce utilizing social sites.

By grasping the understanding to stay associated with customers, many businesses have developed different methods of adapting to maintain an increasing presence.

Mobile and Wireless Technologies: Examining D-Airlines

D-Airlines have implemented a perfect model for using mobile and wireless technologies that serve the needs of their patrons. Some of the techniques that D-Airlines have applied to mobile and wireless technology is to offer value to their customers include mobile recharging locations distributed throughout their airport terminals, in-flight Wi-Fi services, and smartphone apps that can boost the customer experience (Writer, 2012).

D-Airlines has developed a mobile application to serve the needs of its customers better also. The app provides access to company services and features such as check-in, baggage tracking, tallying checked baggage, and an option to view boarding passes. The mobile app has efficiently reduced the need for customers to access customer service representatives allowing them to be available for more daunting tasks.

By applying mobile technology and anticipating the customer's service needs, D-Airlines has been able to institute an online based relationship that allows for communication twenty-four hours a day. By migrating to this mobile platform, D-Airlines can lower costs associated with customer service assistance and provide that service through the mobile application and social sites. Some customers remain the same while reducing labor costs. This is an active process of directing business because it allows service representatives to assist customers in areas which demand more attention.

The benefit of providing mobile and wireless services is that there is an articulated focus of duties to essential processes. The mobile app is a service designed to help the customer, but it is also a system of automation. D-Airlines has implemented a stable platform which frees up organizational tasks to allow the ability to focus on more critical processes which might not be as efficient.

Mobile and Wireless Technologies: Examining V-Airlines

V-Airlines entered the mobile and wireless technology market with a somewhat altered approach. Beginning in December of 2011, the British airline broadcasted that their new Airbus A330 planes would be equipped to send and receive mobile phone calls while in flight (Robertson, 2012). This technology was made available to V-Airlines consumers through AeroMobile. AeroMobile is a communications company that focusses in providing wireless service to airlines around the world.

In attempts to endorse other business adjectives while creating a more significant experience for its customers, company V implemented an iBeacon experiment at one of their airports. By using iBeacon technology, company V was able to direct customers to have their boarding passes ready when they are nearing a security check. The iBeacon technology also advertises offers for goods and services as customer's walk past multiple airport vendors. Along with advertising, passengers can become aware of entertainment discounts before they board. The iBeacon technology allows the company to provide tailored services to consumers as they navigate through the airport. The head of e-business development at company V quotes "we will know who you are and we will know what your favorite cocktail is, and we can have one waiting at the bar as you walk in," (Ranger, 2014).

Efficiency

D-Airlines is more resourceful at applying technologies, but I believe V-Airlines has excellent ideas with enormous potential.

D-Airlines has provided many mobile and wireless technological services as charging stations, mobile apps, and in-flight Wi-Fi which does not imply innovative but rather efficiency. These services are excellent but lack creative vision. D-Airlines is highly efficient at implementing the right technology and making it accessible to all customers. This pervasive strategy has made D-Airlines among Fortune's "2014 World's Most Admired Companies," and ranks first among the world's most admired airline companies for the third time in four years (Cederholm, 2014).

Operational and Enterprise Systems

D-Airlines has a lead V-Airlines due to their business age. D-Airlines began dismantling many of their business functions which were created in the sixties back in 2001. Applying a fresh enterprise system renovation every few years has allowed D-Airlines to support new and trending technology that passengers need. By having an integrated solution already in the plans, implementing applications only require minor with minor attention. Which in turn, helped D-Airlines to integrate the new technologies seamlessly.

V-Airlines began overhauling in 2012. They started by looking to integrate cloud technologies for their solutions. The enterprise system that V-Airlines was researching to implement directly supports wireless and mobile technology.

Both companies implement operational and enterprise systems to assist their employees and consumers. Both have also demonstrated how mobile and wireless technology can improve the customer experience and have performed adequately through strategic planning of their ERP's.

[Insight]: Wireless and Mobile

The terms "mobile" and "wireless" are often used interchangeably, but in reality, they are two very different concepts applied to modern computing and technology.

Mobile and wireless are two separate technologies but are significantly used together. Portable devices are mainly incorporated into the classification of mobile. A mobile device is designed to be taken anywhere. Because of its design specs, an internal battery is usually needed to operate and must be linked with a cellular network that can assist to send and receive information.

Wireless is entirely different. One example is the use of a browser in a local area network where the router traffics data wirelessly. Mobile and wireless systems accomplish different things. While wireless systems provide fixed or portable endpoints with access to a distributed network, a portable or "mobile" system offers all of the properties of that d network that can go anywhere.

Mobile and wireless technology have contributed significantly to the rise of social media activity. The ability to access information, communicate with others or large groups, and increase productivity are all attributes of the increase. Businesses use mobile devices for productivity seamlessly with office technologies. From accessing spreadsheets to developing, mobile devices add to productivity. This trend can affect communication among managers, employees, and how organizations promote and control their organization. It can also distort what boundaries there are between home and work.

[Insight]: Conduct and Ethics

The main reasons why green computing should be part of any is that Green computing benefits the environment. Decreasing energy usage from green practices turns into lower carbon dioxide emissions. Sustaining resources means less energy is necessary to produce and use.

Ways that IT organizations can reduce:
- Utilize energy efficient appliances and equipment
- Only use resources when they are required
- Implement a recycling program

Location information of users is a valid concern regarding security. Tracking of employees seems to be a violation of privacy and a cause for lawsuits. Many software products that track employees are designed to catch malicious activities, but monitoring workers during off-work hours could be violating laws.

[Insight]: Fraud and Risk Factors

Four fraud risk elements escalate a company's exposure to fraud.
- High level of trust in personnel without adequate oversight to verify that they are not stealing from the company
- Relying on informal processes of control
- The belief that internal controls and fraud inhibition systems are too expensive
- Allocating a wide range of responsibilities for each employee giving them opportunities to commit fraud

The most important factor is having a high level of trust for your employees. Proven and trustworthy employees are less likely to commit fraudulent acts. Employees have access to areas and information which could cripple a company. Assigning a wide range of duties for the employee's giving them the opportunity to commit fraud can be countered by establishing authoritative approval levels across the company to serve as an entity-level control, or assigning individuals working within a specific function limited IT access as a process-level control. These types of controls, supported by appropriate segregation of duties, assist in the first line of defense in fraud prevention.

The realization of any fraud prevention program depends on its constant communication and reinforcement. Accentuating the existence of a fraud prevention program through a wide variety of media posters, bulletin boards, and articles in internal and external communications gets the message out to both internal and external communities that the company is committed to preventing and deterring fraud.

ERP integrates all departments and roles across a business into a single information system that can serve each department's particular needs. Many small to mid-sized manufacturers believe that they can do without an ERP, which is not the case. Software companies design their ERP systems to support specific industries. As customers are added, they learn industry best practices and incorporate them into the software. By implementing an ERP system designed for your industry, you automatically make your business processes more efficient.

[Insight]: Visualization Technologies

Data visualization is a great way to convert data into visual graphics that can be interpreted and easily understood. Many companies require essential data which can be interpreted and utilized quickly. An example would be a significant amount of excel sheets containing stats. The presenter is not going to show these vast amounts of sheets but will present them a graph which summarizes the data. This method saves resources while also optimizing efficiency. A great example of technology that is used for data is heat maps. They compare heat indexes around the globe to show acceptable or unacceptable risks dealing with temperature changes.

Many rely on cellular phones to obtain data quickly. It is also imperative to have data on risk management actions that include network security. Essential security data needs to be transferred mobile which then can be easily translated into useful information. Split-second decisions can save an organization from losing critical components to its operation.

Business leaders need to be able to access and interpret data in real-time to make highly knowledgeable decisions quickly. Information and the capability to decipher and act on it has become competitive. To identify new business opportunities ahead of competitors, business leaders require the need to access, evaluate, comprehend, and move on data faster and more effectively than ever before.

[Insight]: Project Management and SDLC

Three critical areas or phases that IT project management must pay attention to are failures to see dependencies between projects, executive support, and poorly designed goals. When the scope and resource allocation are not well-defined, the project can't end well. Time management is vital for any plan to ensure the project runs smoothly.

When different teams develop components, and they fail to see dependencies that exist, joining elements can become difficult. These challenging times require the need for team collaboration.

The first stage is the most vital stage of the lifecycle. The first stage makes the requirement clear; one must understand the problem and understand the technical options for the systems including issues that may occur during development.

When the scope of the project comes in sight, scope creep can appear implying the project will not close as planned. Even when there's a clearly defined scope, one should still be aware of scope creep. Although scope creep is not the only bad thing that can happen, it does have the farthest reach. Without a properly defined scope or allowing changes along the way, a project can go over budget, miss a deadline, and hinder success.

IT Strategic Plan: Exploring Cab Technology Platforms

Introduction

Company U is a convenient, inexpensive and efficient taxi service. It is a location-based app that makes hiring an on-demand private driver easy. The application was developed to assist customers in need to obtain transporters in their immediate area so they can get to intended destinations. The company began in 2009, and now offers services available in over fifty-three countries and more than two hundred cities globally.

Uber's main goal is to deliver rapid and affordable transportation alternatives. The app has drastically cut down on drunk and distracted driving and has given those who do not have an automobile another doable solution to get around. The company has also created millions of jobs around the world.

Today, Company U is one of the prominent transportation services in the world. The company is valued at $17 Billion give or take and is a once in a lifetime success story that usually only comes around once in a decade. Company U was the first of its kind, but once the world adapted to its ease access, transportation will probably never go back to its old ways. Company U has became something great, and the company seems to keep improving.

Technology and Security

The Company U application implements mobile technology with a cloud-based infrastructure. Along with data direct from the customer and location information, the application is able to deliver solutions to consumers. Data science is also used to interpret and analyze the large collected amounts of data. By doing so, they can see trends and adapt adequately to customer's needs. The collected and analyzed data is actually embedded into its application, creating better end-user experiences for both users and drivers. The application enables drivers and customers to interact with each other in a matter of moments. The software is designed to discover riders by using GPS locations provided by their mobile devices. Using technology to connect their employee's with potential customers has given them a competitive lead. With less options being capable of supplying a demand on notice, riders seem to only have a couple of options, and one is sometimes pre-loaded onto their mobile device. The Company U platform only uses technology to connect or allow drivers and riders to communicate.

Like any company just starting out, Company U has had its issues even though security is one of its main goals. With new technology comes new risks, One issue that has executives concerned is cyber security (68 percent said this was their top technology-related worry) (Castellano, 2016). Company U continues to develop safety measures for their employees, customers, and their information. The company requires all employee's to pass thorough background checks as well. Large amounts of funds have been spent to make sure appropriate internal control and data security is implemented to protect all data. The company also trains employees on privacy and data security. Technology will always create opportunities for risk, but as long as proper planning and policies exist, events should be minimal.

Personnel

An involved team is needed for an organization to be successful. The riders are the most important characteristic of Uber's achievements. A team has to be in place to guarantee that the riders are pleased with services being rendered. Customer satisfaction can be a very extensive and intricate process. Different wants and needs will be required to satisfy individuals, different teams and plans being implemented to help ensure customers are satisfied would be well suited as a solution.

Software Developers design, test, implement, and code the different applications or sites. Usability evaluation and user interaction design are two key activities in the development of an interactive system (Skov & Stage, 2012). By incorporating a software developer into the team, we can develop ways to guarantee consumers are satisfied with the applications. Along with collected data, Company U can tailor the app to fit the customers needs. If an issue arises, the software developer can tackle it hands on and look for stable solutions. The GUI is very important regarding its ease of use. Without proper design, it could degrade the functionality and popularity it has with its customers.

An ERP is a system that links internal applications and external business processes. With enterprise resource planning systems, managers will be able to project potential problems that would affect efficiency. ERP systems promote organizational discipline through constraining users to follow prescribed processes and by limiting access to transactions to specific organizational roles (Maas,

Fenema & Soeters, 2014). The system would also provision business functions and processes. The system will also provide the ability for a quick turn around and response which increases productivity and is able to offer assistance to customers.

The CRM System is a business strategy that separates and manages customers to increase customer lifetime value. This system is significant to continue success. The only way to continue to be successful is to have revenue and growth. If the company can successfully manage interactions with its customers, they can grow in profits and revenue. Customer relationship management can help implement effective marketing strategies that will attract new customers while satisfying their old customers.

Security Administrators are responsible for the integrity of databases and networks. They make sure no threats from inside or outside of the business can gain access. It is very imperative to have a security team in charge of protection of the customer's data. If consumers feel as if the integrity of their personal information can be compromised, they will be less likely to use your services. A team tasked with creating and implementing policies ensuring proper practices are followed is logical as well. Security breaches and any events are to be handled by the security teams or administrators. Security is one of a customers main concerns when using products or services.

A project manager is responsible for planning and organizing the completion of IT goals. The project manager will help guide new systems and rollouts to help the company develop. The company will need a project manager to help manage funding and projects schedules. With the help of IT tools and a properly trained team, managing tasks can be tackled quickly.

SWOT Analysis

One of Uber's main strengths is that is the first of its kind providing services this way in its industry. They have developed an application that is efficient and dependable in a small frame time. The management and support operations seem to work well and are team motivated. Their teamwork as dedicated employee is another strength that they. They can set their own standards due to the unique path they have chosen to use technology. With only one other company, which basically followed their lead, there is no comparison to judge them by. They have the opportunity to fix any issues or try different things without disrupting regular operations. They have recently went into food delivery in certain cities. Finally, Company U has its customers on their side. The services provided are well received by the consumers, so they are always looking for the next upgrades to service.

Weaknesses exist. Also, there are some improvements that could be made. The Company U app has been surrounded by popularity, but there have been a lot of negative stories in the media. Many taxi services were not happy about the competition which is quite understandable. Secondly, an attack on the system may have compromised fifty thousand employee's information at risk. The most serious cases that have affected Company U are rape allegations. Due to the lack of proficiency and still being a young company, they haven't had the great success when dealing with the media on these issues.

The mobile application has altered the way individuals get from one place to another, but the opportunities are boundless. There were rumors that the company may get into logistics which shows how flexible their platform can truly be. Company U has the means to create new services and explore new markets.

Many adversary companies are trying their hand at implementing mobile connectivity and transportation services. Because of the use and ease of technology, Company U has to keep an eye out for threats in their industry. When rival companies enter the industry, Company U has to reflect on their prices, so they maintain their customer base but still gain profit. Since Company U is a technology company, having their information compromised puts the wellbeing at a great risk. Malicious hackers and viruses are all real threats that could affect business and are taken very seriously. The company is responsible thousands of drivers and consumers information. If data is compromised, they will lose revenue.

Strategic Plan

Strategic planning is a series of processes a business chooses to help keep its organization successful. Strategic planning as a discipline is relatively young and has gone in and out of favor several times since its widespread adoption starting in the mid-1960's (Cervone, 2014). All successful companies will need to have policies that properly plan for unexpected events. The company should have plans setting forth their path for a very long time projecting them into the future. Management should be planning possible new partners along with events would like to sponsor. One of the most common errors executive leadership can make is to assume that it can delegate the process to others. While it is important that planning be distributed throughout the organization, the top levels of the organization cannot take a back seat during the planning process (Cervone, 2014).

The next step should consist of figuring out how new resources should be obtained. As the company continues to grow, there will be a need for more funding. Market to a new audience or selling more different types of services could serve very useful during these times. Every organization has to decide what resources to share. In order to take the business to greater levels of success, they will have to consider partnerships or joint ventures. Partnering with other successful technology companies can be favorable to the business. Company U must constantly remind the competition that they were the first to use technology in this manner in the transportation industry and their main goal is to stay number one.

Many ways exist that Company U can maintain competitive advantage. Inspiring its customers to stay with them rather than going to the rivalry is a tried and true method. Acquiring customer loyalty is everything in today's business ventures. With the help of new technologies and social media, information can be spread quickly over great distances. If you gain loyalty from a customer, word of mouth and consumer to consumer interactions will fuel your marketing strategy. Company U is distinctive due to its use of technology, and there has never been anything like it before. To keep customers interested, they will have to keep creating new services and marketing ads to appeal to the end user crowd. If a business can assure efficient services all of the time, it is really hard to compete with. Once all issues are properly addressed, safety issues secured, the company stay leading in its industry.

BIBLIOGRAPHY

A Look Back at the Target Breach | Huffington Post. (n.d.). Retrieved from http://www.huffingtonpost.com/eric-dezenhall/a-look-back-at-the-target_b_7000816

CASTELLANO, S. (2016). Be Afraid, Be Uber-Afraid. TD: Talent Development, 70 (2), 20.

Cederholm, T. (2014). Why Delta Airlines Scores Highly on Customer Satisfaction Surveys. Retrieved from http://marketrealist.com/2014/06/Delta-airlines-scores-highly-customer-satisfaction-surveys/

Cervone, H. F. (2014). Improving Strategic Planning by Adapting Agile Methods to the Planning Process. Journal of Library Administration, 54(2), 155-168. doi:10.1080/01930826.2014.903371

Chaudhuri, S., Dayal, U., and Narasayya, V. 2011. "An Overview of Business Intelligence Technology," Communications of the ACM (54:8), pp. 88-98.

Geddes, B. (2014). Advanced Google AdWords. Hoboken: Sybex.

Hardy, M. (2014). Target Store Data Breaches: Examination and Insight. New York: Nova Science Publishers, Inc.

Hsinchun, C., Chiang, R. L., & Storey, V. C. (2012). Business Intelligence and Analytics: From Big Data to Big Impact. MIS Quarterly, 36(4), 1165-1188.

https://www.ibm.com/analytics/us/en/industry/retail-analytics/

https://www.techopedia.com/definition/26418/data-analytics

Maas, J., Fenema, P. C., & Soeters, J. (2014). ERP system usage: the role of control and empowerment. New Technology, Work & Employment, 29(1), 88-103. doi:10.1111/ntwe.12021

Pessi, K., Magoulas, T., & Hugoson, M. (2011). Enterprise Architecture Principles and their impact on the Management of IT Investments. Electronic Journal Of Information Systems Evaluation, 14(1), 53.

Ranger, S. (2014). Virgin Atlantic Tests Apple's iBeacon at Heathrow. Retrieved from http://www.zdnet.com/article/Virgin-atlantic-tests-apples-ibeacon-at-heathrow/

Riley, M., Elgin, B., & Matlack, C. (2014, March 13). Target Missed Warnings in Epic Hack of Credit Card Data.

Robertson, A. (2012). Virgin Atlantic Now Offering In-Flight Mobil Service from London to New York. Retrieved from http://www.theverge.com/2012/5/11/3014873/Virgin-atlantic-aeromobile-in-flight-phone-service

Skov, M. B., & Stage, J. (2012). Training software developers and designers to conduct usability evaluations. Behavior & Information Technology, 31(4), 425-435. doi:10.1080/01449290903398208

Strnadl, C. F. (2006). Aligning Business and IT: The Process-Driven Architecture Model. Information Systems Management, 23(4), 67-77.

Turban, E. (2012). Information Technology for Management: Advancing Sustainable, Profitable Business Growth, 9th Edition.

Writer, S. (2012). Delta Airlines Named Top Tech-Friendly U.S. Airline. Retrieved from http://news.Delta Airlines.com/Delta Airlines-named-top-tech-friendly-us-airline

Yang, Jia Lynn, and Amrita Jayakumar. "Target Says up to 70 Million More Customers Were Hit by December Data Breach." Washington Post. January 10, 2014. https://www.washingtonpost.com/business/economy/target-says-70-million-customers-were-hit-by-dec-data-breach-more-than-first-reported/2014/01/10/0ada1026-79fe-11e3-8963 b4b654bcc9b2_story.html.

Available Now!

Information Technology & Insights: The Erudite Collection
Access Controls Vol 2.

Coming September 2018

**Information Technology & Insights: The Erudite Collection
Auditing Controls Vol 3.**